www.socialanxietyinsideout.com

SOCIAL ANXIETY

INSIDEOUT

HOW TO RISE
ABOVE THE NEGATIVE
CHATTER AND LIVE LIFE
WITH CLARITY

BY STEVE LIGHT

"If reading these pages uncovers the wisdom of just one person, so that they find their own way, then this guide would not have been written in vain"

Steve Light

CONTENTS

MY PROMISE

I promise that reading this guide will make a difference in your life. My intention is to leave you feeling lighter and hopeful that you really can overcome feelings of social anxiety and become the confident person that you've always wanted to be. When I say confident, I mean true self confidence. The kind of confidence where you'll be the same *you,* but will feel happier in your own skin, and importantly when I say overcome, I mean that you'll realise that there is nothing *to* overcome.

The more you read this guide, the more you will gain a deeper understanding of what I am alluding to. When you start reading, don't try hard to grasp what I am saying intellectually, read it with an open mind and without judgement. I know this may feel a bit difficult at first, as whenever we read something, hear something on the news or listen to someone talking, we automatically judge what we hear through our mental filters and create a decision, based upon that.

I'm not saying that critical thinking isn't important, it's very important to question and analyse things in life. But for now, leave the critical judgements on hold. What I am about to tell you is common sense and true for every human being on the planet. When you get this deeper understanding of what I speak of, it may well come in the form of an 'Aha' moment, where you will get an insight (a sight from within) about what I am saying.

For example, have you ever been given advice in life? I'm sure at some point you have! No matter how many times the person told you what to do; it just hasn't felt right to you. I know that has happened many times in my life so far. You know what they're saying is probably right, yet you feel slightly defensive and ignore the advice. Then at a later date perhaps, a thought pops into your mind and you suddenly have a realisation, a feeling that you should do the thing the person told you to do. The reason it feels different this time is because it came from within, a powerful insight that you know deep down to be true.

What I am about to share with you in this guide is a field of psychology known as innate wellbeing, the three principles, health realization or psychology of mind.

Trust me, I care about you, I have been where you are right now and I wouldn't wish it on anyone. Read this guide with an open mind and positive things will start to happen, from within…

"Come to the edge.' 'We can't. We're afraid.' 'Come to the edge.' 'We can't. We will fall!' 'Come to the edge.' And they came. And he pushed them. And they flew." **Guillaume Apollinaire**

THE PROBLEM

What is social anxiety disorder?

In a nutshell, the way I see social anxiety disorder is that it's a fear of social situations, of being judged negatively, combined with low self-esteem. It usually manifests itself in childhood but it can also appear in a person's teens, twenties, and even later.

A rough estimate of the population that is affected by this issue is 1 in 10. Social anxiety can prevent people from doing the things that the majority takes for granted, like speaking on the phone, going shopping in the supermarket, finding a job - and many other situations that involve being in public or involving social interactions.

It can affect a person on many different levels. For example, a person could be feeling anxious at work, taking part in meetings and giving presentations. On the other hand, a person may be fine at work and dread any social gatherings with colleagues, or social interactions outside of work.

It has only recently been classed as a 'mental disorder' since the 1980's, and believe me, it can ruin lives. I have 'been there myself' and I don't want anyone else to suffer with this.

The problems I discovered in 'overcoming' social anxiety disorder (or any other related problems for that matter) are that we are often in the mind set of "I can't do that because X".

We perhaps read about someone who has gained a lot more confidence and overcome social anxiety issues and we think it's not possible for us. We say "It's ok for them, they had extra help, or more money, or fewer issues than me" or even disbelieving that they had social anxiety in the first place! That was my experience and I'm sure many of you will agree.

I used to look at people who appeared outwardly confident and envy them. This included celebrities, successful business people, coaches, and people on the street. I had a lot of anger and frustration inside of me and a longing to be loved and accepted as a member of society. I felt inferior and totally helpless; I couldn't imagine myself being happy. It's so sad now looking back at how I felt.

I found an appropriate term that seemingly fits; it's called 'Learned Helplessness', and was coined by Martin Seligman, father of Positive Psychology. In a nutshell, it's the learned ability to feel helpless, you feel stuck in a state of apathy and feel like you can't be bothered to try anything, as you simply think it won't work.

This is similar in a way to riding a bike. Once you learn how to do it, you just do it naturally and automatically. It's exactly the same with your negative thinking, you have picked it up from your surroundings and it has become habitual. This is the case for so many people and this really saddens me. However, there is hope…

THERE IS HOPE

When you're ready to, I want you to understand that negative thoughts are not you as a person, or anything wrong with you, they are just negative thoughts and feelings bubbling up from the past.

You may think that this is the way you've always been and you'll always be like this.

I can look back and realise that's not true, and I can say the same for many others who I have met and helped over the past 7 years.

Your negative paradigm (view of life) is not set in stone,
You can be happy and have peace of mind,
No matter who you are,
No matter what you've been through,
Innate wellbeing is inside of you.

There has been a big misunderstanding in the nature of thought. That negative thoughts are something to be ashamed of, to suppress, or to even analyse. All of this negative thinking is being stirred up in our minds and it's in the way of our wellbeing.

We think that our happiness and peace of mind is something to strive for, or in something outside of us. We often think that it's found in the future, and when we get there, all will be perfect.

Innate wellbeing means that we are all born happy, with a balanced mental health, but we build up perceived layers of negative thinking. These layers create our negative view of the world. The good news is that we have a choice whether to listen to these negative thoughts or not, so they no longer have to control us.

You'll be relieved to know that there are no techniques to follow in this guide. The words I write in this book are from the heart. I had suffered with debilitating social anxiety for as long as I can remember and have found a way to see things differently. I always knew deep down that there was something else out there other than the many techniques that I had tried on my journey.

I look forward to sharing this understanding with you.

THE RESULTS

I have gathered a selection of quotes from people who have been suffering with various mental health issues and have discovered this new way of thinking for themselves:

"Understanding more about the operating system behind my experience of life has made a huge difference to my life. My experience of meetings at work and other situations where I felt pressure before has totally transformed. This understanding will give you access to new possibilities for your own life and access to the peace of mind and resilience which is available to you behind any current perceived insecurity or self-doubt."

Andy Smith

"I spent the first 23 years of my life living with social anxiety, shyness, insecurity and depression; I thought this was who I was. I developed eating disorders which came with feelings of self loathing, guilt and a huge amount of sadness and isolation. After years of suffering, I came across an understanding of the nature of thought. Within 3 days I felt free, I felt healthy and I knew what I wanted to do with my life.

There are no words to explain the change that took place deep within me, I know that as I sat and listened I did not fully understand what was being said, but I started to experience peace, and I knew that I was not broken. I knew that I was not born shy, or anxious or depressed. I had made up who I was, and then lived out of it without knowing. I realised I was not my thoughts, I was something much greater, I was part of the bigger whole, and nothing in life could change that."

Jenny Anderson-Kennard

"In my late teens & early twenties, the anxiety was so acute that I stopped socialising. It was debilitating. After coming across this understanding, I experienced a period in which I had clarity of mind. My thinking slowed and there was room for insight and health to bubble to the surface. I had the realisation that my anxiety was being created through a belief I held about life; a belief that 'life is difficult and a struggle'. I felt like the plug was pulled and the anxiety went spiraling down the drain! I had psychological freedom, I saw how I was creating my 'anxious' experience.

We aren't broken or in need of fixing; we are simply experiencing thinking which keeps us stuck. Take heart that beyond this thinking, there is access to innate health and intelligence which will guide you toward peace of mind & psychological freedom."

Tony Fiedler

"A few years ago I woke up to the fact that I was not well. All I knew is that it had something to do with dealing with the death of my son. I was trying to raise

my baby daughter whilst wrapped in a suffocating cloak of anxiety and fear; my smile had vanished.

I became mentally and physically exhausted. I saw danger at every turn and was always looking over my shoulder for the next disaster. A nurse friend who, on a walk with our children, asked one simple question that was to blow my whole world open: "What are you thinking about just before your energy drops?" "Huh? My thinking affects my energy levels?" Out of curiosity, I started looking at my thoughts. Sure enough, there it was: I would have a freaky thought, about the world/ my child's safety/ my to-do-list. I would believe the thought; dwell on it and then BAM! my energy would plummet through the floor. My thoughts were indeed at the very root of my well-being.

Then I discovered a description of how this all worked and I could, finally, give up my fight with my thinking. I awoke to the understanding that thoughts are simply a projection – they are only a story that I continuously create about the world. I now know that I can walk my path free of fear and anxiety."

Tammy Furey

"For years - ever since I was 17 years old - I experienced anxiety - sometimes to the extremes that my body would seem to shut down. About 20-30 percent of the time, the anxiety levels were so high that it contributed to painful digestive disorders. This made it difficult to work or be physically active. In 2010, I slumped into a deep depression, experienced many days in which I no longer wanted to live, was collecting disability assistance from the government, and was enrolled into a government sponsored 'anxiety and depression program.' Reading the internet one day I started reading about 'health realization' and since then my life has changed for the better, in ways I could have never imagined. My levels of happiness, connection to others, and sense of peace around others is AWESOME. Compared to just a few years ago, I barely recognize my life."

Gordon Faulkner

"Having suffered from depression for a number of years and tried various ways to overcome it, working with this understanding really has been a complete revelation. It was as though I've found the depression off button! I can honestly say that over the last 12 months I have never felt better."

Ruth J

MY OWN STORY

My earliest memories included two traumatic events involving being in public with people. The first was at the age of 2 when I was on holiday with my parents in Blackpool, in an amusement arcade. One moment I was happily walking along beside them and I must have stopped to look at something. The next moment I was all alone and I started to panic, looking around frantically for my parents amongst the giant, busy arcade. I remember being found by the security guards and I was crying so much that I couldn't tell them my name or my address. I was panicking and I couldn't calm down, I wanted to see my mum and dad so badly. They called out on the tannoy and my mum came rushing. She must have been extremely worried herself and although the whole ordeal felt like hours passed, in reality it was probably a few short minutes.

The second event, just a year later was on holiday at a children's disco with my dad. I was looking out onto the dance floor and there were so many children playing, running around and making a lot of noise.

My dad tried to encourage me to go and join in but I resisted and resisted and started crying my eyes out. I felt petrified of interacting with the other children and I can still remember that feeling all these years later. I think the thing that hurt most was my mum's reaction when she turned up later on. I told her that dad tried to get me to play with the other children and although I'm not sure exactly what she said, it was along the lines of, "Oh, never mind". No sympathy, no cuddle, nothing. Of course, I don't hold this against her at all, there's no way she could have known the extent to which this small event could have affected me.

A few years later, I was the stereotypical shy boy. I would blush a lot, I kept myself to myself most of the time and had only a handful of friends. Reading out loud in class, or any kind of group interaction gave me a strong feeling of anxiety and butterflies. I was a happy child in general, but felt a bit like an outsider.

It was more of the same during primary school. I was pretty much content, but still felt nervous a lot of the time. I loved drawing and I proudly created a poster for our class's ice cream sale but to my horror, I had to go round to each class' and speak about the ice creams that we had for sale. I just couldn't do it, so I took my extroverted best friend Lee along and he happily did it for me when I held up the poster. Thanks Lee!!

Things started getting tough at secondary school (age 11+) and having to adjust to a new school, a new way of learning, new people, new friends, new teachers, new everything! I felt sick in my stomach every morning before school with a fearful feeling almost every day. I was bullied for being fat and quiet. I was an easy target, due to my appearance and because I didn't say much. It hurt me deeply when I was constantly picked on and I felt like I couldn't tell anyone about it due to fear of the bullies finding out. I was too shy to tell my parents and my friends were too nervous to stick up for me. Every registration period I would get picked on because of the way I sounded, it felt so painful, like my heart was broken every single day. I felt so helpless, I tried to laugh it off but it was relentless and eating away at me.

Things started to get a bit better when I was 13; I had grown from 5 foot 6 to 6 feet tall in a couple of years and lost about a stone in weight. I was picked on still by a certain group of people, but it didn't bother me half as much as it once did. I still didn't like my voice but I felt a lot more confident physically and I started to take interest in fashion and clothes. I remember buying some blue suede Kickers shoes (Hello Elvis) and feeling like I finally fitted in with everyone else, it was a great feeling.

Going from lower secondary to upper secondary, things got a bit easier for me, I started to fit in a lot more and got a bit more confident, I was still being picked on by the same guy, but I just thought to myself "He's not worth it" and I didn't let him get to me. I started to get a little bit cocky sometimes and would misbehave in class just to get attention. I was hiding from the fact that I was totally anxious about communicating in traditional ways, speaking out in class, reading or participating in debates. It was all still very much a terrifying experience for me and I avoided most types of activities.

I remember the time when I was in a religious education lesson sat with my mate Simon. We had to describe what or who we thought God was. Simon and I had to join two girls in the class, Anna and Rachel; I asked to go last and sat there, quivering, as the trio took turns to say what they felt about the subject. My heart started beating like a rabbit being chased by a dog, my palms were soaking wet, cold and greasy, I frantically rubbed my trousers to try and dry them, my mouth felt as dry as a pine cone on a hot summer's day. Oh no, it was my turn to speak! "Urm, well, I think God is… urm, yeah, that, I think, urm, well…" I jabbered on. The girls started laughing and as I turned to my right I saw Simon sniggering away at me, I felt worthless and humiliated!

Sixth form was a lot more laid back than school and I started to feel a bit more relaxed. I didn't do too well in my A-levels though, as I dropped out of 3 of my chosen subjects and got a C in Design and Technology. In hindsight, I think I was always trying to tick the academic boxes, whereas I am generally more creative and practical. Maybe I thought I had something to prove, who knows?

I started drinking with friends more and more as I got older and a particularly hard task that I had to perform, was the ordeal of ordering drinks on a night out. The idea of it made me feel on edge. When it was my turn to get the drinks in, I would keep rehearsing in my head over and over and start to doubt myself. I would think that I'm going to say the wrong thing. This would go hand in hand with a constant fear -

which was my lack of assertiveness eating away at me. 'Overly confident' people would turn up at the bar (after I've been waiting patiently for 10 minutes) and would be served drinks straight away. This simply reinforced my beliefs that I was a useless person.

After completing the sixth form, I was too nervous to go to university. I remember vividly looking at different university websites and worrying about how I would fit in, meet new friends and living away from home. It's amazing how a person's thinking can stop them from doing something that many take for granted.

I ended up working in warehouses, building sites and factories for a year or so, as I simply couldn't imagine myself working in an office environment. At least in a warehouse I could keep myself to myself. One day, whilst working at a postal office, I was sat round a table with my colleagues (feeling quite nervous may I add). I was finding it hard to join in with conversation, when all of a sudden on the radio, there was an advert that I will never forget. It was like it was speaking directly to me and it said "Do you feel nervous in social situations? You may have social anxiety disorder". There I was, feeling nervous in a social situation; I felt a glimmer of hope, I was so eager to find out more…

So when I got back I went on my PC and searched for Social Anxiety Disorder online, and came across a forum site called SAUK. I discovered that roughly 10% of the population have this particular issue and for the first time ever, I didn't feel so alone.

It was so great knowing that I wasn't alone. But then I started to think about social anxiety disorder a lot. I felt as if only people who had social anxiety disorder understood or cared about me and no one else did. My world became small and I would spend a long time chatting on forums to people and feeling disconnected from the real world. I started to feel overwhelmed in regards to what next step to take, so I plucked up the courage to go to my local GP.

I felt so nervous about bringing this subject up with my doctor. To help me explain, I brought a printout regarding social anxiety. Admittedly I expected a more empathetic response from him after I had been revealing my deepest, darkest issues. I felt that he responded rather rudely saying that he'd never heard of the problem before and he will refer me to a counsellor, and that was that. (Looking back, I can see that he couldn't know everything, and he did the best that he knew how to do under the circumstances).

I saw the counsellor twice, it was nice to be able to talk about my issues face to face for the first time, but I felt incredibly uncomfortable and decided not to carry on, as it didn't seem to be helping. Perhaps it was my impatience, or maybe I was ready to move on?

I managed to pluck up the courage to enroll at my local college to study a HND in Multimedia. It was something I was interested in, as I had a love of art, design and computers; it seemed like a lot of computer based work and less of the team work, presentations or role playing. How wrong was I? We had to do a lot of group work and a presentation at the end of each module. I would run out of class every time the tutor mentioned that we had to take part in group discussions and even often leave my bag there in the class room.

The idea of giving presentations really freaked me out and I skipped every presentation we had to do. Fortunately, I had a really empathetic tutor who allowed me to present one to one with him after class. On one occasion, I decided to give a group presentation, as I felt it would be easier than doing it alone, we could share the responsibility, and perceived embarrassment.

We stood up in front of the class of about 20 people and my two fellow students started off the presentation and all was going fine. It all started to go wrong when it was my turn to read the last section. I was looking at the board right in front of me, but I just couldn't get my words out. I felt faint, my mind went blank, and I froze. I apologised and said that I couldn't do it. It was so humiliating and it left me feeling like a total failure, I felt like the only one there who was so petrified of giving presentations and participating in group activities.

THE TURNING POINT

A couple of years later, in 2005, I got to the stage where things started to change for the better. It was a real turning point in my life. I was so sick and tired of feeling anxious and depressed all the time. I was missing out on a lot of things in life and felt a real urge to do something about it.

Here's an excerpt from my diary at the time: (Pages 30-37)

Monday 3rd Jan 2005:

The starting point of my recovery. I went back on the Social Anxiety Self Help site for the first time in nearly three years (those past three years just flew by; I didn't really have a life as such, just an existence. Don't get me wrong I had my fair share of good times but as equal amount of bad times, if not more, i.e. going through college being scared of people, being petrified of doing class presentations, being scared of attractive people of the opposite sex....etc.. If you have SA, you will know what I'm talking about).

Anyway...Back to Monday....A really miserable day (and the weather), I was really depressed, I was thinking to myself "what a freak I am" (even though I knew I had SA nearly 4 years previously and that there were loads of people like me, I still felt Isolated, alone and afraid. I went food shopping with my mum down the local high street, my mind was feeling 'closed'. I was safe driving in my car and I didn't want to leave it, so I dropped my mum off and I waited nearby in my car.

She finished in the supermarket and got back in the car. We proceeded to another supermarket and I felt 'safe' as it was a smaller store and went in (felt a bit on edge but not too bad). I managed to help with the shopping and then back home (My safe-haven).

Later on that day I met this great person through one of the SA sites that had come along way getting over the 'mind-crippling mental disorder' that's called Social Anxiety. She showed me some material and was very sympathetic towards me and helped start thinking positive. She even asked me to email her my life story and how SA has affected me (haven't had the time yet, but I will soon). She seems like an amazing, caring person who wants to pass their knowledge of getting over SA, to others.

Wednesday 5th Jan 2005:

Went to the gym early, was in a grumpy mood, come home from the gym, went on the SAUK site again etc…. then I had a mad urge to tidy up, so I really went for it, got all of the clutter out (this is good for me as I rarely keep things tidy for very long), played some loud music while I tidied, music that I rarely listened to. Don't stop me now" by Queen and "Help" (appropriately named) by The Beatles worked well for me to get me in a positive mood, anyway, I was getting things tidy ("cluttered house, cluttered mind" *don't know who quoted that?* but it's true). Normally I am too fatigued and low to tidy up, but I forced myself and I felt tons better!

Thursday 6th Jan 2005:

Today was the best day of all, I read the success stories on the SAUK site (try it!), they inspired me so much, I felt for one of the first times ever, that there was hope, hope that I could beat my SA. I even felt slightly more confident today, I was on a natural high, stayed in my room most of the day still but I applied for at least 30 jobs on-line today (as I am a New Media Designer who can't work in his dream job due to SA and a lack of commercial experience). I am currently unemployed at the moment because I usually feel 'trapped' due to SA, I don't know what job to go for, Working in a shop is a big NO! Not a chance in hell of working in customer services. I can't work anywhere that I have to talk directly with people. So I usually go for manual labour types of work, warehouse etc…. where I don't mind the work, It's just that I get really anxious when people approach me and try to make conversation with me as I can't hold a conversation for very long, you all know what I mean.

So that never lasts long at all... I either walk out of work or get sacked for 'not working hard enough' (because I am unhappy). My girlfriend doesn't understand this, she just thinks that I am plain lazy, which, from another person's point of view might seem right. How are they supposed to know if you don't tell them what's going on in your mind?

I tried working in an office about 2 months ago, I was so chuffed that I got the job! (me, work in an office, never?). My first day there wasn't that bad actually; the anticipatory anxiety kicked in as natural that morning, all the usual questions went through my mind, *what will the people be like? Will they like me?* I took a deep breath before going in and everyone seemed nice, I was doing filing, so I didn't have to deal with people: phew!

I felt more and more isolated as the days passed so (in fact I was only there 2 days, Tuesday and Wednesday). I decided to call friends while at work - must have called 2 or 3 different people a couple of times to tell them about the new job and to say hey (wasn't too long on the phone), just so I would feel safe again (I called them outside of the office in the corridor).

I got the sack on the Friday Morning. My car broke down and I phoned in to explain. The job agency that I worked through said "Oh, don't bother coming in as your services are not required" - it was because I had used my phone. I was devastated to say the least; I got sacked because I used one of my many 'defence mechanisms' at work due to having SA. It wasn't my fault, but what can you do?

Back to Thursday... I played basketball this evening, had a good time, tried talking more and be more involved by keeping score and trying to joke with my mates. Come back home, feel really positive about beating my SA, I haven't ever felt this positive, no matter how stupid, weird or inferior this story would sound to non SA sufferers, this really is my first big step, and I'm over the moon!! I have started thinking clearer and changed my perspective on life slightly too, in a positive way!!

I'm only 5-10% closer to my goal, but it's a start.

I strongly advise all you fellow sufferers to get together with other fellow sufferers whenever you can. I haven't yet, but my next step is on Monday evening where I am going to a support group in Bristol and hopefully to the pub afterwards with a few of the members. If there is anyone local who wants to come, please let me know and we could go together to the group.

I can't believe how much I have written!! I have been at it non-stop for 2 hours 24 minutes (it's 2:24am now). Better go, got to get up and go to the gym for 9 o'clock in the morning!

I hope this success story is inspiring to you as the others were to me. Remember, be positive. You will get there in the end. "Step forward to beating your Social Anxiety and don't look back."

I made it along to the support group the following Monday and I knew things were going to get better from now on; this was my time to take control of my life. Meeting other people who understood how I felt was a breath of fresh air.

Every session I attended, I met new people and slowly started to believe in myself. I met a girl called Emma at the group and we became good friends, we supported each other through 'overcoming' our feelings of social anxiety. Only a month before that, I had been thinking there was no hope. (Just as a side note, be open to things working out for you, and they will. I didn't go to the group to make new friends, it turned out that I made a good friend. Don't force anything; don't take it personally if you don't make friends when you meet people, there's no point in trying too hard to make a friend. People will like you for who you are, not what you're trying to prove to them).

After a few of the group sessions, I felt ready to move forward onto something else, something a little more challenging. I came across Paul McKenna's NLP training; I was intrigued that I could learn how to create positive habits in myself and others. The course was 1 week long, with 300 attendees in total, so a big challenge, but I felt ready to face my fears.

About a year after I originally booked on this course, the day arrived. The fact that I left my comfort zone that day and got myself out of the flat and en route to a course was a good feeling, although I was doubled up with anxiety, the usual "What will happen? What will I say to them? What if I forget what I'm talking about?" was running through my mind on the tube to West Brompton. I felt physically sick at the thought of sharing a room for 7 days with 299 other strangers; it terrified me to say the least!

I entered the building, I got there very early to avoid any extra stress on top of the already overloading amount of anxiety I had in my body. I sat down on the sofa and a lady was sitting opposite, reading a paper. I think I shakily said "Are you nervous?" to her, "Yes" she replied "You?" "I'm absolutely shitting myself!" I gulped. We got chatting, and as we were both very anxious, we connected really well and spoke about why we wanted to do the NLP course. We got on really well and the remaining 20 minutes flew by and it was time to go in.

It was a beautiful large hall with high ceilings and lavishly decorated. I started to feel really excited and to get a sense of why I was there, ready to indulge myself fully into the NLP training. I was sat in my seat, trying very hard to make conversation with the people either side of me. I managed to talk for about 20 seconds to one person, but that was about it. All of a sudden, the lights dimmed down and some really upbeat music starting blaring from the sound system, "Ladies and gentleman! Please create a warm welcome, to your host, Paaaaaul Mckennnnnnnnaaaaaa" the voice boomed across the airy hallway. I felt electric; Paul came from the back of the crowd, through the middle and up on to the stage.

After the introduction, we had to speak to at least 3 people that we hadn't met before, I felt a bit more upbeat and a little bit more familiar with the environment, so I went over to chat to a few people separately. This one guy, Kevin, one of the helpers came up to me and introduced himself, "Hi, I'm Kevin, nice to meet you" he said in a über-confident, laid back manner. We got chatting and it turned out that he once was a sales director for a large international company and is now a therapist in Harley Street, I was impressed by his history and he seemed like a cool guy, so I got his business card.

The next day I bravely submitted my request into the requests box to Richard Bandler, as I wanted him to help me with my social anxiety. So he read out my request in his bold, Dennis Hopper-esque, American accent *"Please help me with my social anxiety"* echoing across the large conference hall. It was the moment that I had dreading since the training started 2 days previously, and I never thought he would have picked me. However, I was full of adrenaline and buzzing like mad, I put my hand up to his request and spoke to him from my near front row seat.

He said to come up on the stage, the audience applauded me as I got up, and I was very nervous but focused and ready. I shook hands with the co-creator of NLP and complimented his funky coloured shirt and heard a few chuckles in the audience as I sat down next to him. Looking out at the sea of people was a surreal experience, it made me feel truly alive, after I had spent a lot of my time isolated... life feels very real in moments like this. I felt on edge and very anxious, but it was generally a pleasant feeling because I felt safe.

Richard proceeded to work his magic on me and put me into a trance. I still had the ability to remain in control of myself and felt conscious, and it was like I was floating, in a total state of relaxation as I sunk back into the comfy chair. There I was, sitting there in a state of bliss as he went through a routine of turning my negative thoughts around. He told me to think of a time where I felt anxious and he asked me to think of those moments by creating a picture in my mind, then to slowly drain the colour out of the image and to shrink the image and shrink it again until it was small enough to stamp on (to reduce the significance of the emotions attached to the incident). It was so clear in my mind and I felt the feelings associated with these anxiety provoking events draining from my mind. It was a freeing feeling, and it was incredible. He then told me to sort through the other times where I felt anxious, making the images in my mind black and white again and to imagine stomping on them until they disappeared.

He slowly brought me back out of the trance and I felt at peace. It felt amazing, like I was on top of the world. I rubbed my eyes in disbelief as I looked at the crowd, I no longer felt anxious, sitting in front of so many people. "Welcome back" he said to me with his mesmerising glare. I felt totally at ease and I thought to myself "Is that it now?" Then Bandler started chatting to the audience about something else unrelated, one of his stories, whilst I sat there feeling totally chilled out and gazing at the crowd.

He then turned to me, held my hand, raised my arm up above my head and told me to hold it there, looking into my eyes he said "Take a deep breath in and relax" then all of a sudden, WHACK! Using the base of the palm of his hand, struck me right in the middle of the forehead and said "SLEEEEP" My head dropped down like a sack of potatoes and I was back in a trance again, full of adrenaline with an intense feeling of relaxation. Again I felt totally conscious of my surroundings and it felt blissful… so great in fact that I was happy staying in this state for a while longer. Unfortunately for me, things had to move on and Bandler slowly counted down 10....9....8....7....6....5....4....3....2....1 "Come back into the room".

I blinked a few times and came back into reality. Bandler asked me "How do you feel about those bad feelings now?" "Nothing at all" I replied, grinning like a Cheshire cat, which was absolutely true. I felt totally clear headed and free. Every time I tried to recall these old feelings, I couldn't, I could remember the events still, but the negative emotions no longer existed.

Time for my exit from the stage. I shook Bandler by the hand and thanked him warmly, I feel unstoppable. I got up and walked from the stage, when he grabbed me by the wrist and said "Hold on one minute" as he pulled me back towards him. He said to me "Go and say something to the crowd" I said "What do you want me to say?" He replied "Say anything you like". I got up on the centre of the stage and said to the crowd of 300 people, "Is everyone having a good time?" The crowd roared and I felt absolutely incredible, it was one of the best moments of my life, it was a real sense of freedom in that moment.

Throughout the rest of the course, I threw myself into it and got up on stage a second time with all of the many people there who had a fear of public speaking and I even gave a video testimonial at the end about how I enjoyed the experience. On the last day I got to meet Michael Neill in person, he's known as SuperCoach, and I really liked something about him, he was very down to earth and just being himself.

I went up to get the lady's book signed who I met at the start of the course, but it turned out that he signed it to me instead! I thanked him and told him how much this course helped me and helped me in overcoming my social anxiety. Our eyes met, I shook his hand and he smiled warmly back at me, such a lovely guy!

After the course, I had a hunger to try other courses and gain more confidence. So, in Early 2008, a friend of mine recommended a life coaching course in London, it was over 3 days with about 150 people. Although a little nervous, I knew that I could do it, as the previous NLP event was twice the size and length! My friend Emma and I attended together, and it really did help boost my confidence further, it was just what I needed at the time.

I went on to do another couple of their courses, but the one that I am most thrilled about was the third program with this coaching company. This program went on for 3 months, consisting of 3 Saturdays and one evening a week and by the end of those 3 months, each individual on the course would have their own community project.

We got to work in teams of 5, and I really benefitted from the support that I had from the others and our group coach, Sue. We supported each other during regular conference calls, brainstormed event ideas and all set our event dates together. My idea was to set up a 1 day social anxiety conference, where people come along to take part in taster workshops. These workshops would last one hour and the participants would get a glimpse into how the therapy or technique works and how it could help. I had a few ideas to include Laughter Therapy, CBT, NLP, Thought Field Therapy and Public Speaking.

Then 8 weeks into the course when everything was going well, I was invited to be interviewed by Ruby Wax regarding Social Anxiety, for their BBC Headroom Campaign. This campaign was fantastic as it looked into different people's lives regarding their mental health condition and how it impacted them. Every week Ruby would interview a different person with a different mental health condition. One week it was Anorexia, then Depression then Bi-Polar Disorder, then Social Anxiety and so on. I was invited to speak about my experiences of having feelings of social anxiety with Ruby.

On the day I was feeling extremely anxious about meeting Ruby as I had an image of her being loud, gregarious, brash and sharp-tongued after seeing her on TV for many years. Oh how my preconceptions were wrong. She was so genuinely interested in what I was saying, made me feel at ease and even shed a little tear when I shared my story with her. It was an experience which I will never forget. After the interview, I asked her if she would like to come along to my event in 4 weeks' time and support the cause and to my surprise, she said yes!

I completed the coaching course, and the first Leading Light event happened on the 22/11/2008. 80 people turned up that day and I was the happiest man alive. Ruby Wax showed her support by giving a short speech during the event and even joining in with the group activities. I could hardly believe that this once chubby, shy kid, now an adult of 26 created this huge event. This was one of the most significant moments of my life. I felt as if it was a huge turning point in my life, even more so than the NLP event 2 years previous.

After the first Leading Light event I decided that I really wanted to help people on a regular basis. So I looked at how I could set up a local support group in London. I had an idea of how a support group is run, from the days of going to the group in Bristol, but apart from that, I had no experience, just a passion to help people like me.

I found a local venue in North London and booked a room for a future date. Then I created a website for the group and people started enquiring about the sessions. At the first one we had 12 people arrive. I was so scared and felt out of my depth, but I was honest that this was a 'support group' and although I wasn't sure on how best to run the group, I really had a passion to help others like myself. The session turned out well and when one person started talking about an issue they had, another would relate to how they felt and the atmosphere was very uplifting and supportive.

That was 4 years ago and I'm happy to say that things have continued to improve in my life since. I still have had ups and downs, but I feel that the big difference now is that I know social anxiety isn't part of me.

The good news is that the lows don't last as long as they once did. I don't let it stop me do the things I want to do, plus I can say no to the things that I don't feel like doing (rather than proving to myself that I can do it).

A NEW SOLUTION

Ok, so now you know a little bit about my background, it's time to talk about the ideas behind this guide.

About 4 months ago I started looking into how I could interview people online, I was still a little nervous talking over Skype but I wanted a new challenge. So one of the first people I emailed was Michael Neill.

I got a reply from Michael's lovely assistant Terri, It read…

Michael Neill <******@*********.com>

to me

Hi Steve!

Michael would like me to send a book to you. Could you please let me know your shipping address? Thank you!

love

Terri

I was so moved by the lovely message but didn't get an answer about the interview date so I sent a follow up email about 2 weeks after and got this back...

Michael Neill <******@**********.com>

to me

Hi Steve!

He would like you to read the book first - then I can get something scheduled in!

love

Terri

"Wow, little old me is going to get to interview Michael Neill" I thought to myself. I was so incredibly excited (and anxious).

The book arrived and I felt really excited about reading it because it was different to Michael's other books that he's written in the past.

I had just assumed that it was an NLP based book, and although I do think NLP has some good points, it still didn't sit right with me. I felt that there had to be a gentler way.

I sent a reply to Terri to confirm that the book had arrived:

Steve Light <**********@gmail.com>

to Michael Neill

Hi Terri,

Aw thank you so much,

I just received the book yesterday and have read it 1 1/2 times so far, it's blowing my mind. It's such incredible work, I had a huge insight into my power and what's possible, it was such a wonderful feeling. Wow...

It's like it came along at the right time, It answers so many questions that I have been asking since my personal development quest started in 2006. I have looked into so many disciplines that I had become massively overwhelmed with it all and feeling worse! Recently I have been down the 'Conversations with God' path, it's so beautiful and I love Neale dearly, but I was totally in my head all of the time.

Then 2 weeks ago I started trying out Tony Robbins' Personal Power II, 30 day course and felt that it was the time for me to go the other way and get on my wealth and achievement path, I stopped after 15 days when my coach friend Janis told me that I have everything I need right now, there's nothing missing... Then Michael's book came along and reaffirmed that!

Thank you so so much Terri and Michael for your kindness,

Looking forward to speaking with you soon,
Love
Steve

The first time I read it I was desperately trying to grasp what he was saying. I saw something in it, but I don't think I fully got it. I persisted with it as there had to be something to this as Michael decided to leave everything he had built up over his coaching career, and move in this new direction. He gave up the old way of working with NLP and has seen something in this way of working that feels more authentic to him.

Then I decided to read it a second and a third time, but this time I put all judgement aside and I really started to understand what Michael was trying to explain.

I wanted to know more so I explored Michael's recommended links at the back of the book. Although this field of psychology was still widely unknown, there were little pockets all over the world. Some people had been using it for 35+ years with phenomenal successes in helping clients overcome a whole host of issues.

I got in touch with a coach by the name of Wyn Morgan just to hear about how he discovered these principles and how it has helped him. He had such a moving story. We got chatting and he kindly offered me a free place on Michael Neill's online course starting in June! I was so grateful that he would do that for someone he'd only just met.

I checked out Michael's video course and got so much from it, especially the community aspect of it. I got to share candidly about anything that was going on regarding my life and what insights I have got through developing an understanding of the principles.

The more I share with the group about what was going on in my life, the more I realised that it was all my perception, it was all my thinking. A positive side effect of this was my resilience to hearing about people's problems. Previously, I would feel fatigued and sometimes fearful of hearing about people's problems. But since, it has become a whole lot easier to listen and empathise without getting emotionally entangled in their negative feelings; it really is wonderful to have that ability. We all have that ability.

I kept having more glimpses into how this understanding could help so many people in the world. I still had down days, but I fundamentally knew that it wouldn't last and to my delight they never did. Something had changed in me, with this understanding of the nature of thought I had a lot more control over my well-being.

The more I think about this understanding, the more I realise that automatic negative thought is illusory; the more comforting it becomes, as it means that I never have to be afraid of my experience. Even at the low points, where the mental pain feels real, I know it will pass. There's a lot of freedom in knowing that there is nothing really wrong with you, it's just that you are habitually thinking negative thoughts.

When these negative thoughts are popping up unannounced, what we usually do is judge them, try to suppress them, get angry at them, feel guilty for having them and we feel like we are slipping back or 'relapsing' for having them.

When we negatively judge our negative thinking, it's like continually shaking up a snow globe, we can't see clearly and it feels like we are actually in a blizzard. The best way to calm down the snow globe is to leave it alone, and it will settle down by itself.

Let me show you the kind of thought patterns I would have regularly:

"I'm feeling anxious again" "I thought I'd cured my social anxiety" "I'm slipping back" "I'm stupid" "I'm a fucking idiot" "Things will never change" "I thought I'd cracked it this time, I was stupid enough to think that I would change, change is for others, not me, I don't deserve it" Then I would be walking around feeling miserable and annoyed at the world!

I would go through 'good patches' feeling confident, then I would wake up feeling crap again, or go to a social event, feel anxious and beat myself up in my mind "Why has the anxiety come back?" "I thought I got rid of it?" Can you relate to this? Do you feel confident one moment, or in certain situations, then wonder why you feel anxious again in others?

This was before I understood the nature of thought. Sometimes I do get stuck in thought again, but it passes. Like today, as I type this, I have been pretty stressed out about money and have been feeling particularly low, but the difference is, I know it will pass, I'm just having a bad day, not "I'm a fucking idiot who is slipping back into old ways and there is no hope" like it used to be.

Michael Neill explains this superbly in his latest book, The Inside-Out Revolution:

> *One of the great distinctions I've learned from the work of Syd Banks is between meditation as a practice and meditation as a state of mind.*

Having spent many years pursuing that state through a variety of religious practices, new age teachings, and technological gadgetry, it was a shock to me when I first glimpsed the inside out nature of the human experience and recognized that meditation – a quiet mind and a beautiful feeling – is our natural state. We can think our way out of it in an infinite number of ways, but the moment our thoughts slow back down, like an electric fan coming to a stop after being switched off, we return to that place of inner quiet and insightful wisdom.

Not long ago, I heard a new description of this natural state of mind from some friends who came to visit. They had just come from an "intensive" where they spent a few days focusing on the thought/feeling connection – noticing that in every single moment we are living in the feeling of our thinking.

When I asked them what they got from the experience, they reflected for a few moments, and then replied "More periods, less commas." (Actually, they're English and they said 'More full stops, less commas', but I thought I'd translate...)

When I asked them to elaborate, they said that what they were noticing was an absence of the running commentary on our experience that usually goes on in the background of our mind.

For example: "I'm upset that they did that, and they need to stop, or else it means that they don't love me."

became: "I'm upset."

And: "I am such an idiot, but that's judgmental, I shouldn't be so judgmental, after all I've been learning all these wonderful things about how the mind works, and I want to be a good person, but how does that work when I do something stupid, am I just supposed to sit here and not beat myself up about it and hope that I'll magically learn not to be such an idiot in the future?"

became: "I am such an idiot."

The resultant quiet they were experiencing in their minds was equivalent to having spent weeks on a meditation retreat, something both of them had done in the past as part of their search for a better and more meaningful life.

Why does any of this matter?

Because the meditative state of mind is the closest thing to a "magic wand" that I have come across in 25 years of exploring the human potential. It heals the body. It is the gateway to our deeper wisdom. It opens us up to a world of deeper feelings. It gives us glimpses into the nature of the universe.

Most people who understand its power have learned to access it through discipline and practice over time. But when you recognize it as our natural state, there is nothing you need to do. It is not only where you are sitting right now. It is the one who is doing the sitting.

HOW THIS FIELD OF PSYCHOLOGY BEGAN

An uneducated welder, a Scotsman named Sydney Banks had a huge insight into the nature of human experience when on a weekend retreat. He was chatting to a psychologist about his insecurities and the psychologist turned round to him and said "You're not insecure Syd, you just think you are"

As Syd Said, *"What I heard was: there's no such thing as insecurity, it's only thought. All my insecurity was only my own thoughts! It was like a bomb going off in my head ... It was so enlightening! It was unbelievable ..."*

This Eureka Moment led Syd to the discovery of the three principles of Mind, Consciousness and Thought.

The three principles are true for all human experience and can be explained as follows:

Mind - the universal energy that animates all of life, the source of innate health and well-being. (In my own words: The miracle that we are actually alive and the unseen 'energy' that surrounds us. Some of us call it divinity, omnipotence, spirit, life force, God, universe, everything. By all means, this isn't exclusively a religious description).

Consciousness - the ability to be aware of one's life. (In my own words: We have awareness of what's going on through our senses).

Thought - the power to think and thereby to create one's experience of reality. (In my own words: We think over 60,000 thoughts per day which shape our view of the world).

You may be thinking, *"What!? an uneducated welder discovered a field of psychology?"* you're right, does sounds a bit far fetched doesn't it? But like I said, put that critical thinking aside for now, and keep looking in this direction. Many mental health professionals are using these principles in their practise with outstanding results. It's not some mystical process, although it may seem that way at times, it's common sense.

THE MYTHS THIS APPROACH DISPELS

Since discovering these principles, I want to dispel the myths in regards to 'overcoming social anxiety disorder'. These are 'innocent myths' of course, it's just that a lot of therapies use old, outdated methodologies. It's not to say that other therapies don't work, all therapies do work for some people, but as this guide points out, change is within, not from the outside.

You could compare it to surgeons in the early 19th Century discounting basic hygiene such as the washing of hands, as it was common knowledge then that disease was caused from bad smells, aka Miasmas.

It seems so ridiculous now in the 21st Century as its common sense to surgeons to 'scrub up' before performing an operation. I'm hopeful that in the not too distant future, people will understand these principles in the same way and they will be commonplace.

Myth One: Social Anxiety is something to cure or to overcome.

I truly know that it feels that way, I really do and I don't say this lightly. There is nothing wrong with you. You don't have social anxiety disorder, you just think you do. So there is nothing to overcome. I'm being brave in saying this because I care, and it's not to say that your experiences and struggles aren't painful, we both know that they really can be.

Social anxiety disorder describes quite accurately how I felt, and still feel at times, in a neatly labeled box. It displays a list of symptoms and potential causes, which is useful in pointing you in the right direction for help. I am grateful for this, as before I discovered the term, I was drifting along, feeling incredibly anxious in life, thinking that this is my personality and it couldn't be changed.

So I'm not discounting mental health diagnoses as they have their purpose. But the bottom line is, social anxiety disorder isn't an illness, social anxiety disorder isn't part of your personality, social anxiety disorder isn't you, it's not your identity, and you are so much more than social anxiety disorder.

Myth Two: You have to analyse your past experience to solve your current issues

I was an expert in pin pointing why I had social anxiety disorder, my parents, genetics and a premature birth featured highly, with a dose of bullying at school for good measure. I know that having these feelings wasn't my fault and somehow, throughout my life, I learned how to be shy, quiet and anxious through the events that I experienced and the meaning that I added to them.

Now with this new understanding of the principles, I realise that there is no need to trawl back through the past and bring up old and often painful memories. That's not to say you should forget the past entirely, the past made us who we are today. But spending years in therapy talking about how I felt when I couldn't find my parents in that amusement arcade, or how being bullied at school affected my self-image, just gets you thinking about the past and bringing up past hurt. It's common sense really, I know it's good to let off some steam by talking about issues, but continually digging up the past is simply reinforcing the emotional effects of the upsetting life events. Would you keep poking a bruise to make it heal? No!

If you kept prodding at it, it wouldn't heal. You simply leave it alone.

Myth Three: It takes many years of facing your fears

I thought this myself, as soon as I hit that turning point in 2005, I thought it would be years of hard work and facing fearful situations before I found the 'perfect confidence'. I'm grateful for all of the experiences I have had to 'better myself' but looking back I was just still generally unhappy and chasing the carrot of 'perfect confidence' that was way out there in the future. Like an unquenchable thirst, I was happy during the courses that I went on but still felt 'thirsty and unsatisfied' when I went home and back to real life.

When you understand the nature of thought, you realise at a deeper level that we are all thinking creatures. Although I feel it's good to do things that you're slightly nervous about as the feeling afterwards is fantastic, you don't have to go out for hours on end and ask strangers for the time, talk to checkout assistants and do other superficial tasks that some therapies suggest.

Myth Four: You have to analyse the content of your thoughts

Many therapies and techniques tell you to keep a thought diary, tell you to keep track of your anxious thoughts, analyse them and re-frame into positive thoughts.

Sounds exhausting!

What is interesting about the principles is that it focuses on the ordinary miracle that *we think*. So it's not looking at the content of our thinking and trying to analyse and reframe, It's pointing to the truth that all humans think, and as Syd Banks said, that's equality right there, we all have mind, consciousness and thought in common.

Myth Five: You have to think positively all the time

Positive mental attitude, can do mindset, positive thinking, were bandied around a lot in the early days of personal development and still are to some extent. The fact is, it's hard work, you keep thinking positive thoughts, which can help, but then you try and fight the negative thoughts when they come up too and it becomes and internal battle in your head.

The same goes for positive affirmations. The most famous affirmation of all time is probably "Every day and in every way, I am getting better and better" I'm not saying that it doesn't work for some people. It's just that I didn't believe myself when I was saying it. Then I felt crappy for not getting any results just seems like a waste of time. You really need to feel it and believe it inside. Going back to the insight, if you suddenly believed and really felt that every day and in every way you were getting better and better, it would feel amazing, it would feel true to you, just as true as how you know that your name *is you*.

Myth Six: You have to be happy and confident all of time

We all know life has ups and downs, but it's time to change the way you look at yourself in regards to being a happy and confident person all the time. I felt that if I felt low after a period doing so well that I was failing, slipping back to old ways and I would be doomed forever.

Even the 'best of us' have suffering, heartaches, down days, and unhappiness. The difference is, when one understands the nature of thought, mind and consciousness, you know that it will pass, that it's just a low mood and not anything to judge or analyse.

Myth Seven: Events in the outside of you effect the way you feel

Life happens to us all. We all experience things, good and bad. Some experience it worse than others. But the thing is, all of the *experiencing* is happening within, not from the events themselves. One example of this is a guy named Nick Vujicic who was born with tetra-amelia syndrome, a rare disorder characterised by the absence of all four limbs. He of all people would get a little credit for living an unhappy life for living with this disability. But he's turned what's happened to him around by seeing it as an advantage and he's inspiring people all over the world. Although this example may seem like an extreme one, it demonstrates the ability that all humans have to overcome adversity.

We all know that each one of us has our own opinions about things, and a lot of the time we think our opinion is the right one. A classic one for men is the feeling of being 'nagged' by their partners, we often have a perception that we're being told off and they are the ones who are in the wrong. In their eyes we are the ones that are in the wrong. We often feel as if our partner is making us feel a certain way, but it all comes from within, their behaviour is distilled and processed through our mental filter.

Myth Eight: People don't understand or care about my problems

"Everything that irritates us about others can lead us to an understanding of ourselves."

Carl Jung

When life was at the lowest points, I had a belief that no one cared or understood how I was feeling. I was totally embarrassed to tell anyone how I felt, and when I tried I couldn't get the words out. Then when I showed my girlfriend at the time, a little booklet explaining social anxiety, she still didn't really understand, as she hadn't 'been there' to the extent I had. Looking back, I knew she cared but I guess she couldn't really grasp what it was all about. It was more about my perception that she didn't care.

I must have radiated this sense of 'no one cares' as I developed a bit of an attitude with some people and saw the world as an uncaring place. All of my bosses were uncaring for firing me because I had social anxiety disorder. The fundamental point here is that the world wasn't the problem, my thinking was the problem, and I *thought* that no one cared. I focused on the negative of the world and that's what my experience became.

There are people out there in the world, of whom you haven't met yet who already care about you; people like me who want to help you. Because they have been in dark places and want to help you, just keep your eyes and your mind open, you never know who is going to help you, they might be just around the corner.

TIPS FOR SUCCESS

Please feel free to re-read this guide as many times as you like. Every time you read it, you'll hear something new, the words will be the same of course, but your wisdom inside of you will present an insight and you will see things differently. You may feel totally different about a paragraph that you read for the second time and now you'll think "Oh, so that's what he means".

- Don't try to grasp anything I have been saying intellectually. An intellectual understanding doesn't do anything for you. It will present itself as in insight, a feeling inside of you; you'll know when you 'get it'.

- Just go easy on yourself, don't force anything, just read with an open mind and let it sink in. Like when you have a nice hot shower, you don't try too hard to get wet, you just get wet.

- The more you fight with your own negative thinking, the more it persists.

If I can sum up *How* to put this into action, I would say this:

When you next have negative thoughts pop up, just observe them and realise that you don't have to listen to them. Don't suppress them, let them be and they will lose their power. Sometimes you may not be able to pin-point a tangible thought and you'll get a negative feeling instead. If that happens, realise that it is still just your thinking

Please remain hopeful. I know that this may not make sense right away because our thoughts and feelings can seemingly overpower us at times. You *will* gain clarity and it will make more sense when you spend a little time calming the mind and remembering what I've said.

Keep looking in this direction and you will open up to things that you never thought possible.

FREE AUDIO DOWNLOAD

What I'd like you to do now is to listen to your free audio download that I have provided. Listen to it as many times as you like. I will be talking further about the principles that have been discussed in this guide.

You can gain access and download right away via:

www.socialanxietyinsideout.com/audio-download

Remember, it's all about you, you know what you need to do. Be quiet and listen...

I'm going say farewell for now, with a wonderful quote from Sydney Banks:

All the best,

Steve

P.S. Remember, this understanding of these three principles is not some magic process to follow. You don't have to intellectually remember what they are specifically. So I would like to put it simply, in my own words for you.

You are so much more than you think you are. Your negative thinking is not you. It's just a negative thinking habit. Every human being learns from their environment, and what most people don't realise is that we are reacting to these negative thoughts that popup all the time. The beauty is that we don't have to listen to them.

There's nothing you need to get/achieve/do to be happy. With calmness of mind comes clarity of thinking. Trust your inner wisdom, your gut feeling, your intuition and you'll find your way.

"Let your mind be still, for the wisdom you seek is like that butterfly over yonder. If you try to catch it with your intellect, it will simply fly away. On the other hand, if you can still your mind, someday, when you least expect it, it will land in the palm of your hand."

Sydney Banks

APPENDIX

RECOMMENDED READING:

There are many fantastic books out there that go deeper into the true nature of thought and these principles. Don't feel you need to go out there and read everything there is to read, just read what feels right for you. I've read a few books now and I've had my own insights from reading about others experiences.

Go to:

www.socialanxietyinsideout.com/readinglist

to find out more...

CONNECT WITH ME:

I'd love to hear how this guide has helped you, so please feel free to get in touch:

Twitter: www.twitter.com/stevelight82

Facebook: www.facebook.com/stevelight82

Email: socialanxietyinsideout@gmail.com

Web: www.socialanxietyinsideout.com
and www.stevelight.org

SPREAD THE WORD:

Before you go: I would really appreciate if you could do 2 quick things for me. To help me spread the word about this guide and create awareness for people who are suffering with social anxiety disorder.

1. Click here to tweet your friends
   www.socialanxietyinsideout.com/tweet

2. Leave a quick review on Amazon
   www.socialanxietyinsideout.com/review

Printed in Great Britain
by Amazon.co.uk, Ltd.,
Marston Gate.